Becoming a *"Transformed"* Woman of God

Be Who God Created You To Be!
21-Day Journal

Belinda Hawkins Sanders

Unless otherwise indicated, all scripture references are from
New Living Translation (NLT)
New International Version (NIV)
King James Version (KJV)
The Message (MSG)

Becoming a "TRANSFORMED" Woman of God
21-Day Journal
© February 22, 2021 Belinda Hawkins Sanders
ISBN# 978-1-953526-08-3

All rights reserved under International copyright law. This book or parts of thereof may not be reproduced in any form, stored in a retrieval system, or transmitted in any form by an y means; electronic, mechanical, photocopy, recording, or otherwise without prior written permission of the publisher or author, except as provided by United States of America copyright.

Published by TaylorMade Publishing of Florida
www.TaylorMadePublishingFL.com

TaylorMade Publishing
904-323-1334

Table of Contents

Forward i
Preface ii
Chapter One: A Mind To Change 1
Chapter Two: Mentor and Mentee 3
Chapter Three: Stand Up and Fight Like a Child of God 5
Chapter Four: I Want to Live 7
Chapter Five: Be Made Whole (BMW) 10
Chapter Six: Get Your Emotions and Mind Untangled 13
Chapter Seven: Stand Up to Your Fears 15
Chapter Eight: A Safe Place 17
Chapter Nine: Sharpen Yourself 19
Chapter Ten: Choose To Be Happy (CTBH) 21
Chapter Eleven: Let Them Talk 23
Chapter Twelve: Go All In 25
Chapter Thirteen: Change Your Circle 27
Chapter Fourteen: Today Be Strong and Courageous 29
Chapter Fifteen: Arise From The Low Places 31
Chapter Sixteen: Rehabilitation 33
Chapter Seventeen: How Did I Become What I Became 35
Chapter Eighteen: Recover 37
Chapter Nineteen: Restore 39
Chapter Twenty: Rebuild 41
Chapter Twenty-One: It Is Party Time 43
Thank You! 45
About the Author 47

Forward

Having read this journal in its entirety, I can assure you that as you read it, likewise, will you be led into a "step by step" process of what Becoming A Transformed Woman looks like!

Belinda, my spiritual daughter, and mentee shares her story with "personal transparency" and as you read through it chapter by chapter you can feel the emotion (even pain), or uncomfortableness often associated with transformation or CHANGE in form or being.

As one who traveled with her on this journey called TRANSFORMATION, I know what Belinda writes about in this journal is something that any woman reading it can find helpful, even life giving. For other women this journal will certainly bring encouragement and a place where they too can journey through their own personal process to TRANSFORMATION!

I'm happy to say Belinda is progressing quite well in her transformation process and has allowed the Father God to turn her "former pain" into great purpose! Enjoy!

Apostle Sharon Peters-Ruff
Sweet Rose of Sharon Women's Ministry
Founder/President

The Strength of Eagle's Wings Global Network, Inc., Founder

Preface

I have learned that in life if there is a cause for change, then you must not just change but you MUST TRANSFORM!!! When you are going through a transformation you will not go back. Remember the caterpillar, once it makes its change (transformation) it will not return to what it used to be. So as a transformed woman there is no going back.

The butterfly will NEVER be a caterpillar again. It BECAME what it was created to be. Now even though we have been transformed it does not mean that other storms or situations will not come. Yes, situations will come, but how we look at them and deal with them will be so different. Because of your transformation, you are not that same person. This journal was created to help you get through your transformation
My prayer is that my transformation will be an example to other women to encourage, cheer, push, coach, and teach them what may seem impossible is possible through God. Even when it is the toughest fight that you've fought, even if it is your greatest fear. At the end you will come forward.

So, enjoy this 21-day journey and challenge yourself to write reflections and notes so at the end you can go back to read them and see how far you have come. Embrace it and allow the process to move you. Transformed is what I became!
I pray this journal blesses you as much as it blessed me as I wrote it.

Chapter One: A Mind To Change

May 9, 2014 was the day that changed my mindset. That was the day I said I no longer wanted to live the way I was living. I was being tormented by not being my best self and instead was living with low self-esteem, going around in the same circle, seeing no change, crying all the time, unhappy, overeating and overspending and the list goes on and on.
At that point in my life, I smiled, and it felt good. Then, I wanted to go from feeling good to feeling FABULOUS AND BEING MY AUTHENTIC SELF.

I had to first stand up and say, "Hey I've got some issues that I need to fix". I had to accept that there were some things in me that I had to change in order for other things to change around me.
The word of God tells us in Romans 12:2 New Living Translation, "Don't copy the behaviors and customs of this world, but let God transform you into a NEW person by changing the way you think. Then you will learn to know God's will for you, which is good and pleasing and perfect."

I understood that my TRANSFORMED mind would cause things around me and in me to change. Bless the Father! Transformed means to change in form, appearance, or structure; metamorphose. (dictionary.com) I knew that I was NEVER going back to the way I used to be. To be honest I did not want to go back. I saw my DESTINY; I saw what I was becoming, and it all started with a mind change.
When I saw where I was headed, I had to begin preparation to adjust how things were done in my life. Each day I kept moving forward.

Challenge Note

Can you pinpoint or picture the time when you had a mind to change? How do you envision your destiny?

Chapter Two: Mentor and Mentee

God will send people into your life to help you. I could not have done this alone. I was afraid and felt I could not do it because of the way I was, for it was familiar to me. God put a strong woman of God in my life, Apostle, Sharon Peters-Ruff. She took me through a two-year mentoring class. Sometimes after class I felt like she was pulling me, and I was screaming, "IT HURTS AND I DO NOT WANT TO FEEL PAIN!" Then, there were days I would scream, "WHEN WILL IT BE OVER?" I had to learn that it was a JOURNEY and a journey it was and still is.

A mentor is a person that will walk beside you to help you get through those tough days, especially when you want to just throw in the towel. The mentor gives you tools that you can use to help you in the journey. The mentor will speak not just to you, but speaks also to your being (within) that reaches your SOUL. For the soul mind, will and emotions must be free with your body and spirit. I am a student that is teachable now, to sound and true doctrine. Praise my Father in heaven for that!
My mentor helped me to see the dark areas within that I did not know were dark. I call it a place of familiarity, a place of comfort. Through the power of the Spirit of God and the wisdom that God gave to her, I was able to see the light that a darkened life had caused me to live in!

I will say to you and anyone else, find someone that will walk a journey of life with you and someone you can be accountable to. Someone that you can trust; for the mentee has to be open to heal. Ruth had Naomi, (NIV) hear her words, "But Ruth replied, Don't urge me to leave you or to turn back from you. Where you go I will go, and where you stay I will stay, Your people will be my people and your God my God." Even when you slip or try to go backwards, the mentor is there praying and cheering you on. As my mentor says to me often, "Daughter Come Forward". Now I say to you my sister...Come Forward!

Challenge Note

What areas in your life do you believe you need help with?
Pray and ask God as you allow the Holy Spirit to guide you that He will give you a mentor that will walk the walk with you on the earth.

Chapter Three: Stand Up and Fight Like a Child of God

That day on May 9, 2014 was my enough is enough day. I had to tell those things that were holding me down YOUR TIME IS UP! Loose me and let me go!

As I stated in chapter one, I was tormented day after day. I did not understand why I was feeling the way I was feeling. I went into depression and suicide mode. I felt like, "what was the use of living and fighting". My mind was tired of the warfare. I had to put on my spiritual garments and fight back! That meant I had to get up when God told me to get up and pray, pray, and pray. Then, I had to spend time with Him and hear what He was saying to me through His word and in my quiet time alone with Him. That meant I had to turn the phone and television off.

I began to realize other people were going through what I was going through. What made my heart hurt was when I overcame a battle, and I knew of someone that was in the middle of the same fight. I felt their pain because I sat in that same seat before. Pain from what you may ask; the pain of life's punches is my answer! However, these old knees got me through many storms.

It will seem as if you are the only one going through it, but you are not and you will get through it. I got through low self-esteem, depression, suicidal thoughts, marriage not working out, my sons doing crazy stuff, family and friends talking about me, should I continue? I think you got my point; we must move on. When you stay in the ring and fight back by Faith, people will start to see the winner that you are.

1 Timothy 6:12 New Living Translation says: "Fight the good fight for the true faith. Hold tightly to the eternal life to which God has called you, which you have declared so well before many witnesses."

I put my Faith in the Father and allowed him to help me.

Challenge Notes

Why do you feel your life is worth fighting for?

Chapter Four: I Want to Live

Life will bring the unexpected! You may be in a place of peace and joy, doing well or so you think, but here it comes... BOOM (the unexpected.) Yes, there are some unexpected things that will arrive or occur in life, but we MUST not allow it to control us. Instead you must get a grip on it!

In life there will be some things that may want to take you out and it will become overwhelming at times. I remember a few times those voices in my head would tell me, "kill yourself, no one cares about you". Those voices would say, "if you want this to be over, then the best way is to kill yourself".

Then came the deeper depression. I felt like I was just here and not living my life. My life was on hold, well that is how it felt. I did not care about myself, bills, or anything! I would go home, shower and just sit until it was time for bed if I were not already in the bed. The only time I felt good was when I ate comforting food.

That was not living. I had to transform those things in my life, yet again. One day I took off of work and I went to the beach (I love to sit near the water and think and talk to my heavenly Father). That day I was saying to God, "show me what I did wrong, can you take this pain away from me, it hurts really bad, I cannot do this, why me Father, why me". As I was on my way home, one of my nieces named Ladonna called me and this is what she said, "Aunt Belinda I was up early praying, and I could not pray for anyone but you. God told me to call you and tell you he sees you". WOW, I pulled over on the side of the road and just began to cry and tell her some of the things I was going through.

I wanted to live, I wanted to see my sons, my grandchildren, my mom and my family and friends. I prayed to God that he would give me the strength each day to not take my own life. I had to fight those thoughts of suicide in my head daily. I stayed in the word of God, and I prayed a lot! He put people around me that were strong in the faith and they did not judge me. In that season of my life I alone did not know how to take control, but by the grace of God I did.

Psalm 107:20 New Living Translation says: "He sent out his word and healed them, snatching them from the door of death".
I am still here, and I owe it all to the Father. I got through it with the word of God and real love from others. Your life is worth living; for it is bigger than what you see in front of you.

Challenge Notes

Write down the things you want to live for and why.

Chapter Five: Be Made Whole (BMW)

Being made whole is a journey. On this journey I learned to exercise my spiritual muscles. In this journey I discovered that I was stronger than I thought I was. Keep in mind that a journey is a journey, and it takes time. I have been at this for years and I'm still on a journey. My journey now is a "clearer journey" headed into a brighter and anointed future. Being made whole is healing in progress. In a book I was reading the author said that miracles are instant, but healing takes time.

No one needed to show me how to be bound. I had that "down pat" as they say in slang. However, I did not know how to be FREE and WHOLE nor how to remain in liberty. I now know these things are my portion to have!

God desires his daughters to be free. He tells us in his word, that Jesus came to set the captives free! I want to speak to your spirit and let you know that the Father sent the son to rescue you and free you.
One of my favorite scriptures in the word is the story in Luke 13:10-17 when you have time please read where Jesus saw the woman in the condition that she was in and it moved Him. He called the woman to Him and spoke to her and said, "WOMAN thou are loosed from thou infirmity".

She was loosed, set free, unchained, and healed, from that which had her bound. Hallelujah! Infirmity is sickness, illness, or disability. Jesus sees you where you are, and He is speaking to that place of brokenness, pain, confusion, darkness, disappointment, and place of violation. The place where you were mishandled, the place where loneliness and abandonment resides.

My sister, you may be in a place of brokenness and you feel it will never end or there is no cure for it, yet; I have a testimony that there is healing for anything that you may be going through. Notice I said going THROUGH because my sister, you will come out. I dare you to find the cure in the word of God. Yes, I did just that!!!! I found it in the word of God, and I began to speak that word day after day until it settled in my Spirit. "There is a proclamation for every problem", quoted by Apostle Sharon Peters Ruff. I may not share the same story with you, but I have a story. I sat in the hot seat. My Jesus came and spoke to that area in my life and I was set FREE. Now I am whole, and I am transformed by the renewing of my mind. My mind is renewed every day through the word of God.

Challenge Notes

Write down all of the things you desire to be whole in. Now take those things to the Father in prayer.

Chapter Six: Get Your Emotions and Mind Untangled

Before I went to counseling, my emotions and mind were all tangled up. They were so entangled it was likened to a spool of yarn. Imagine that you are looking at some yarn, look at the strings on it, now take three strings and knot them up and now begin to untangle it. That is how my mind and emotions were, in KNOTS, entangled and twisted.

I remember in many of my counseling sessions I would always ask, "Am I crazy"? That is what it felt like. I felt as if I were about to lose my mind. I was always wondering this and that. I wanted to make decisions but did not know how. I was only believing what I saw. I was allowing my emotions to lead me. It was day after day full of confusion.

I wanted to be WHOLE!!!!!!!!!!!! I called out to God to help me stop feeling this way and let me be free. Jesus asked the man at the pool of Bethesda in John 5:1-15 (please go and read it); WILL THOU BE MADE WHOLE? Again, he asked the man did he want to be made whole. So, let me ask you, do you want to be made whole?

So many people know how to be bound but only free people know how to be free and REMAIN free. Galatians 5:1 is my deliverance scripture. It says, "Stand fast therefore in the liberty wherewith Christ hath made us free, and be not entangled again with the yoke of bondage." You MUST guard yourself and remain in your freedom at all times.

I wanted to be made whole.

Challenge Note

Write down the things that you want God to make you whole in.

Chapter Seven: Stand Up to Your Fears

I had allowed fear to control me. It had a hold on me where I could not see past what was in front of me. You may ask, didn't you believe in God? Yes, I did but I did not believe that God would work for me. Fear did not allow me to move forward. I could not see the other side. What if I am wrong? I would say to myself, "I'm going overboard". I kept thinking if I do not do something then I am going to remain in this same state. I had to stand up to fear and tell it, ok you have got to GO!!!

That day I felt so good I was light on my feet. I finally stood up to fear and I am sure fear is fearful of me now. I fasted, prayed, and stayed in the word until I got a breakthrough. Bless the name of God!

So, I arrest the spirit of fear by receiving the love of God and everything that comes with it. 2 Timothy 1:7 says, "For God hath not given us the spirit of fear; but of power, and of love, and of a sound mind." (NKJV)

Challenge Notes

What fears have you overcome?
Know that you can help someone else overcome their fears!

_____
_____
_____
_____
_____
_____
_____
_____
_____
_____
_____
_____
_____
_____
_____
_____
_____
_____
_____
_____
_____
_____
_____
_____
_____

Chapter Eight: A Safe Place

Often, we must remove ourselves from the place that hurts us so that we can heal correctly. For me, I had to separate myself certain situations so that I could see clearer because I had to fight the strong thoughts of suicide in my head. I knew I needed an exit plan!

I thank God I was able to go to a place where I could have peace of mind. It was a place where no one knew who I was. A place where I was loved. A place where I grew in my spirit and mind. I had to sit back and be a "student", learning how to take control of my own life with the guidance of the Holy Spirit.

In that safe place I began to find my strength. Even strength I did not know that I had. I was able to laugh and smile. Even though my mind would wander back to old things at times, I had the strength to see it for what it was. This assured me that I was on the right path. God surrounded me with people that were stronger than me to help "stretch me" and help "nurture me" spiritually. I was in a safe and secret place with God and I still abide there.

Psalm 91:1 He that dwelleth in the secret place of the most High shall abide under the shadow of the Almighty. (KJV)

Challenge Notes

Have you ever felt unsafe? If so, when? How did you get out of the unsafe space?

Chapter Nine: Sharpen Yourself

In this transformation season in my life I knew things around me would have to change because there was a change that was happening within me. I had to work harder at what I was doing. I had to brush up on my skills, take better care of myself. I got plenty of sleep because I knew I had to be refreshed day after day.

Staying in the word of God and looking over my notes from my sessions was a must for me. This is what kept me in peace. I had to find what it was I was feeling in the word of God. One day something came against me and it did not affect me at all. I was so thankful to God for I knew I had been transformed into ANOTHER WOMAN!

I did not want any setbacks. So whatever I learned I put those things to work on my behalf. I even made sure I took some certification classes that would help me, and they did. I was godly proud of me! I had applied Philippians 4:13 to my life that says: "I can do all things through Christ who strengthens me."

Challenge Notes

Write down the things that you need to sharpen up on.
What is your action plan?

Chapter Ten: Choose To Be Happy (CTBH)

I made a choice in my life... and that is to be happy. I Choose To Be Happy! I took that stand to be happy. Now I did not just stand up, but I started moving making bold moves that lent to my happiness! I was being TRANSFORMED by the RENEWING of my mind. I was not that mad black woman, sad woman, depressed woman, for that is who I was in my past. I took a stand to become a Happy Woman!

In December of 2018, my mother at the age of 90 years old died. Before she died, she took my hand and looked me in my eyes and said, "Belinda, you make sure you take care of yourself." WOW, her words went right into my soul. I believe that it was God speaking right through her to me. Those powerful words empowered, and motivated me to do just that.

Positive energy is very healthy for one's mind, body, and soul. It will fuel you even the more. So, make happiness a part of your life each day and watch how you start growing.

Challenge Notes

What moved you into your happy place?
Define your happy place!

Chapter Eleven: Let Them Talk

For years I was affected by what people said about me. If I heard something, I was one that wanted to hear the whole thing. Craziness, yes, I know! That was because of the strong insecurities that were part of my being. I always felt I had to over explain why I was doing what I was doing or over speak on why I disagreed with something.

As I began to get stronger, it did not bother me anymore. Now it may draw some concerns but truly little concerns, especially if it is negative. I came to realize that people often tend to care more about what's going on in the lives of others rather than minding their own business!

So, I said, "I must be special", so I gave them more to talk about. I continued to better myself and I got to a point that their words did not affect me any longer. I just let them say what they wanted to say! I gave it over to God. I stayed focused and did not allow my emotions to be attached to their words. I continued to become who God created me to be.

Challenge Notes

What has affected you? How do you overcome the negativity of others?

Chapter Twelve: Go All In

Have you ever worked on a project and you put everything in it? Well that is what you are going to have to do for your life. You've got to go all in. You've got to put everything you've got into YOU. We are good at investing in many things and other people, however; often we do not invest into ourselves or our own lives!

If you do not invest in you, then you are an empty vault. There is no investment in it. Believe it or not there is so much worth on the inside of you that money cannot buy. You are so precious to God and the investment in you is for others to gain from. Note: you have a treasure in you in accordance with the Word of God.

Hear the scriptures: "But we have this treasure in earthen vessels, that the excellency of the power may be of God, and not of us." 2 Corinthians 4:7 Therefore, I had to learn that in Psalm 139:14 it tells me that I am fearfully and wonderfully made by the Father and so are you. We have purpose and the clock is ticking. So go and give it the best that you have! Throw yourself all the way into your transformation! A better you awaits!

Challenge Notes

What are you working on that requires the best you?

Chapter Thirteen: Change Your Circle

The hard part for me was to change my circle. Since I was being transformed, some did not understand, or they did not like the transformed me. If they were not causing me to come up, then my relationship with them had to change. I did not feel I was better than them; however, in this season in my life, I needed people to help me move forward not backward. I needed people that were seeing what I saw. I needed people who would correct me and not those who wanted to hurt or wound me. I needed to be around people that motivated me to keep going and not stop.

So yes, my circle changed and so will yours. I began to pray and ask God to surround me with the people that I am called to, surround me with the people that were sent to help me and those I am supposed to help. Please know such people are out there. God will bring them forward to connect with you and your life.

Challenge Notes

Examine your circle!
Who is in it? Name them one by one and analyze their purpose!

Chapter Fourteen: Today Be Strong and Courageous

Let's read what God told Joshua in Joshua 1:9 New International Version, "Have I not commanded you? Be strong and courageous. Do not be afraid; do not be discouraged, for the Lord your God will be with you wherever you go."

Have I not COMMANDED YOU (Belinda), to be strong and courageous? Now you can put your name in there. Now COMMAND is a direct order and BE means to EXIST. So that means God has given a direct order that strength and courage exist in you. My sister, we must not allow the Spirit of fear to be in charge, we MUST raise up, level up, and mount up! Put your BIG GIRL PANTIES on along with the complete ARMOR OF GOD to operate with the strength that God has given to you. I know, yes, I hear you are saying you cannot do it. I said the same thing. You are going to have to reach way down within yourself. Trust me, it is in you. Everything that you need is right there inside of you.

Now listen to this, whatever you may be going through or becoming, if God thought that you could not do it or make it, he would have not allowed you to go through it. I heard that in my soul. So, as you are carrying this thing, know that you will not break. Now you will "bend", but you will not be broken. Come forward, others are waiting for you. Come on and cross over your "Red Sea".

I discovered that I had some strength and courage that I did not even know was there. Those things that once were like a giant to me, now became small. I can stand up to it and no longer allow it to belittle who I am.

Challenge Notes

Write down some areas that you need to be stronger and more courageous in!

Chapter Fifteen: Arise From The Low Places

In becoming transformed, we must remember to stay in the light. I understand that our minds sometimes think about what we went through, but do not stay in that place. Sometimes those places will cause confusion, guilt, and recurring pain. We should thank God for bringing us out; however, our deliverance is in the light and not in darkness.

He delivered us OUT of darkness and into the wonderful light. 1 Peter 2:9 tells us, "But you are a chosen people, a royal priesthood, a holy nation, God's special possession, that you may declare the praises of him who called you out of darkness into his wonderful light." (NLT)

I remember when I would think about those places, I would ask God to help erase those areas that brought me great pain. Yet, I could think about them and smile and give Him praises for where He brought me out of. I was able to stand against fear, giants, and places I felt insecure.

Stay true to yourself my sister! Some days I was down and some days I was up, then some days I just did not feel like fighting. Even though I did not have suicidal thoughts during those times, my strength felt weak. I will say again and again that my faith in God had grown deeper and He gave me that strength I needed in that time.

Challenge Notes

Write down the things that you can truly say you have overcome.

Chapter Sixteen: Rehabilitation

I was talking on the phone one day to one of my spiritual sisters, Pastor Aretha Green, as I was checking in on her because she had surgery on her shoulder. She said something to me in conversation which was, "Pastor Belinda, it is not the surgery, it is the 'rehab' that is the hardest for me!" When she said that, it hit my spirit.

Rehabilitation is to restore to a condition of good health, or to bring back the ability to work or the like. Bringing back or (restoring) to the original condition as it was before the accident or incident happened. As my Apostle would say, "I feel God right there"! We know in rehab, they work the area that is wounded, or the area affected or not properly working. Just as in rehab, we are to work on the areas that have been wounded, broken, or bruised so that they can be brought back to function in their original state.

Do not forget that God is there taking you through every step of the way. Hear the scriptures: Exodus 3:14, "God said to Moses, I am that I am." Let the Father be to you what you need during the rehab sessions and for life!

Challenge Notes

Write down the process of your rehabilitation!
Take Note of the hard parts!

_____
_____
_____
_____
_____
_____
_____
_____
_____
_____
_____
_____
_____
_____
_____
_____
_____
_____
_____
_____
_____
_____
_____
_____
_____
_____
_____
_____
_____
_____
_____

Chapter Seventeen: How Did I Become What I Became

I sometimes ask myself, how did I become what I became in some seasons in my life? For example, how did I allow someone to control my mind which in turn caused me to have low self-esteem? I also became so weak in my mind, yet before then I was NOT weak. If we are not careful we can easily become something that was not a part of the plan of God for our life.

I am the daughter of the Most High God. I stopped fighting and giving into the old me and put all my fight into my future. When I saw a glimpse of who I was becoming, I fought even harder. Yes, I got knocked down multiple times. Yes, I cried all over again, but I kept hearing and believing in the word of God.

The process was something I thought was unbearable. Jesus! However, this woman right here, named Belinda; the daughter of Isaiah and Betty Cole can honestly say she stood the process. The only way the process was going to do what it was designed to do, was for me to go through it being assured that everything has an end date attached to it.

I really did not see at the time; it was causing me to develop. All I knew while in my process was that I was in pain day and night and I was confused. Yet, I desired to live the life that God had for me. His desires became my desires and I stopped fighting the process. So, let us continue to desire his ways. I learned the outcome will be that you become who you were created to be on the earth.

Come on butterfly, let us be transformed.

Challenge Notes

What has God Created you to be on the earth?

Chapter Eighteen: Recover

Let me say this out loud, YOU WILL RECOVER!
Re-cover in dictionary.com means to get back or regain something lost or taken away, to REGAIN a former and better state or condition. For we know God created us (MANKIND) in his image Genesis 1:27. However, as I call it "life issues" came and we allowed things to happen that we really had the power to stop. I know in my own life I did not use the God-given power nor strength in me to stop things I could have.

Sometimes I got angry and I did the opposite of what I taught my children to do or what the word of God says I should do like "be ye angry but sin NOT." I allowed things to build up on the inside and at times I would blow up and my MOUTH would get to moving and my hands would start moving - I mean it was like hot cakes.

Your recovery season is like a wound that has been deeply covered up with a band aid. When you pull it off, the pain comes back alive, but when the Father pulls the bandage back; He is causing healing. The pain has kindled so that the wound can be completely healed leaving only scars that do not hurt. I had to recover to regain myself. Let me stop right here and take a breather!

I did not just want to recover THINGS but recover MYSELF to being in a better state and condition. So, during my transformation I was up and down a lot of times and it seemed like that was becoming my normal. I knew that it was not healthy, nor was it safe for me. However, I am grateful that the Father has re-covered me. I was covered from the old and transformed and re-covered with the new. Glory to God!

Challenge Notes

Allow the Father to re-cover you by reviewing the old and the new YOU!

Chapter Nineteen: Restore

Let us look at the word Restore.

Restore in dictionary.com means to bring back to a state of health and soundness, or vigor. During my transitioning, I must be real and say that I went through mental breakdowns, point blank! I needed not only to recover, but I needed to be restored back to health.

Look at these synonyms for restore; FRESHEN, RECHARGE, RECREATE, REFRESH, and REGENERATE. I needed all of these. I was a broken wall in need of repair to the fullest. Ezra and Nehemiah were instrumental in the restoration of the city of Jerusalem after captivity. They prayed and fasted to see a breakthrough.
Ezra 8:23 says, "So we fasted and sought our God for this, and He was moved by our prayers".

Listen, you must get into the presence of God. For me, yes, I prayed and fasted and allowed God to move. I sought out God, let me say that again, I sought out God. I needed my Father to come and restore His daughter back to health. Praise Him for He did just that. Always remember and never forget it is a process and it is necessary for you to go this course.

Challenge Notes

Do you see yourself being restored? How?

Chapter Twenty: Rebuild

Ok, you have recovered and been restored and now it is time to REBUILD. I envision someone sitting on a chair with a wheel of clay. Reshaping the clay then reshaping it over again until the maker was satisfied with what he made.

That is just what God is doing when he is rebuilding you. He is rebuilding you in the way that he wants you to be. Jeremiah 18 talks about how God told him to go down to the potter's house. The potter was working at his wheel and his vessel. The vessel of clay that he was making was spun in his hand and the potter REWORKED it into another vessel that seemed good to him.

There is a saying that says, "Jesus take the wheel". Yes, allow him to rebuild what was restored and recovered. The rebuilding will have a stronger foundation and you will be strengthened. When life throws you stones pick them up and let God rebuild your future.

Challenge Notes

What are the areas that must be re-built in your life?

Chapter Twenty-One: It Is Party Time

I celebrate you today! Listen, your transformation is for the glory of God. It is the best for me and for you. Now walk in your true authentic self. Yes, it is the REAL you, now you are ready. There is a song that comes to mind by McFadden and Whitehead, "Ain't no stoppin us now, we're ON THE MOVE"!

Let the glory of the Father show up. In John Chapter nine, Jesus saw a blind man. His disciples begin to ask questions about who sinned in his family that caused him to be blind. Jesus said to them, the man nor his parents sinned. This happened so that the works of God might be displayed through him. Come on Father! Let the Father be displayed in you my sister.

As my mom would say, "Gone Now"! So, I say to you, "gone now woman of God"! Walk in the door, this is the other side that has been awaiting. Look at all those people celebrating you and have been waiting on you. Go right in, look around, it is your celebration!

Psalm 91:15 (MSG) says, "Call me and I'll answer, be at your side in bad times; I'll rescue you, then throw you a party. I'll give you a long life, give you a long drink of salvation!"

Challenge Notes

Write down how you plan to celebrate!
You deserve one!

Thank You!

I start first by saying, I acknowledge this as the Lord's doing. I give Him all the glory for this assignment. Thank you, Father in heaven. I want to say thank you to my mother, Betty Cole, while on her death bed she spoke life into me during an extremely hard time. Those words felt like Jesus was speaking right through her. I would like to acknowledge Isaiah Cole, my daddy, for your love, support, and my upbringing.

I want to thank my left and right arms, my two sons, James and Jameel. You were always there for me even when you knew how hard times were for me. You did not judge me but spoke encouraging words or did encouraging things to make sure that I was smiling. I love both of you deeply.

Thank you to my siblings; Anise, Debra, and Dennis and my entire family for the love and support that you have. To my two best nieces, First Lady Ladonna Allen, and Tytina Sanders-Bey, you are the world's best nieces. Thank you for the late-night texts and calls and the deep conversations that were motivating. Tytina thank you for sharing your stories that gave me hope that I can get through this. Ladonna your prayers, resources, and the pushing of the word is WHY this transformation must take place.

Thank you to Apostle Sharon Peters-Ruff, my mentor first, who later became my Apostle/Pastor. You got right down in the heat with me. When I said I can't see it done or I can't do it, the power behind the wisdom that you spoke to my soul, spirit and my life always lifted me up. Words cannot tell how grateful I am for you. I know that I was two hands full during this process, but you stayed right there with me. Then you pushed me out of the nest.

Thank you to my sister circle of coaches and mid wives that helped bring about this transformation. A very special thank you to Pastor Beverly Wilson, Pastor Monica Lloyd, Prophet Frizella Taylor, Apostle Deborah Nicole Delaney, Latonya Cox, Sherita Booker, First lady Jamesetta Scott, and Linda Wells. I want to say thank you from the bottom of my heart.

Each of you played a big part in my transformation. Some of you experienced the same thing I went through, and your presence and talks helped me get through many, many tough nights, and confused mindsets. I saved the best for last, my grandchildren; James, Jada, Jayden and JaVell. Granny loves you so much and my prayer is that my true self wants to help you become your true self in life.

About the Author

Pastor Belinda Hawkins Sanders is a called Woman of God who loves the sheep, an Intercessor who is committed to prayer and teaching the word of God. She is known for her dynamic Bible teaching. As a triumphant woman who has overcome much, her message of hope transcends socioeconomic and denominational barriers and allows her to preach the Gospel of Jesus Christ with power, impacting people  from every walk of life! Transformation or "change" is something that she submitted to by way of a divine process that was needful to renew her mind to know and recognize the good, acceptable, and perfect will of God!

Pastor Belinda is the CEO/President of "Talitha Women's Nonprofit Organization", where their motto is: "Rising Above It All". Talitha is a ministry that was birthed through her to minister to women and young adults to help them reach their greatest potential in life.

Pastor Belinda attended Chicago Baptist Institute. She was licensed and ordained under Apostle Daniel Wilson and she has completed several ministerial certifications.

In an effort to be strengthened in the faith and equipped for her NEXT, Pastor Belinda aligned herself with Unveiled Ministries, an equipping center for leaders where they can be trained and developed for their higher calling. Under the mentorship of Apostle Sharon Peters-Ruff, she has mounted in spirit as she has likewise experienced healing and restoration as it is God's plan for ALL believers.

As a passionate, gifted, exhorter and motivator; the core of Belinda's message is "Be strong in the Lord and in the power of his might". Ephesians 6:10, for truly it was the hand of God that kept her through her many struggles of life. Pastor Belinda is a recipient of God's loving kindness and she likewise extends that and mercy to all who need it.

The heart of God is engrafted in the heart of Pastor Belinda and the heartbeat of her care and concern is for her biological family and her spiritual family whom she loves dearly!

As the times grow worse and the day of the Lord approaches, Pastor Belinda draws nearer to God's word and communes daily with the Holy Spirit. While holding tightly to the promises of God, she joins the likes of many who she co-labors with to the win the lost for Christ!

She is the youngest sibling out of fourteen. She is the mother of James and Jameel whom she loves dearly. The Grandmother of four; James, Jada, Jayden, and JaVell, she is also the Godmother of Jasmine Allen.

www.ingramcontent.com/pod-product-compliance
Lightning Source LLC
Chambersburg PA
CBHW072039080526
44578CB00007B/534